LEADERS WHO WIN, LEADERS WHO LOSE

The Fly-on-the-Wall Tells All

Nancy R. Daly

ScarecrowEducation
Lanham, Maryland • Toronto • Oxford
2004

Published in the United States of America
by ScarecrowEducation
An imprint of The Rowman & Littlefield Publishing Group, Inc.
4501 Forbes Boulevard, Suite 200, Lanham, Maryland 20706
www.scarecroweducation.com

PO Box 317
Oxford
OX2 9RU, UK

British Library Cataloguing in Publication Information Available

Library of Congress Cataloging-in-Publication Data

Daly, Nancy R., 1959–
  Leaders who win, Leaders who lose : the fly-on-the-wall tells all / Nancy R.
Daly.
    p. cm.
  ISBN 1-57886-147-0 (pbk. : alk. paper)
  1. Leadership. I. Title.
  HD57.7.D345 2004
  658.4'092—dc22

                                                              2004002978

∞™ The paper used in this publication meets the minimum requirements of
American National Standard for Information Sciences—Permanence of Paper
for Printed Library Materials, ANSI/NISO Z39.48-1992.
Manufactured in the United States of America.

To Michael and Ryan for their love, patience, humor, and understanding. They are my touchstone from which to spread my wings to experiment and fly. I am forever grateful.

CONTENTS

PREFACE

Leadership is a combination of instinct, personality, and learned skill. While we can't do a whole lot about someone's instincts, we can create awareness of the positive and negative aspects that personality brings to a leadership moment, and we can learn by example. That is the purpose of this book: To share experiences through candid real-life stories that result in learning from other leaders' deeds and misdeeds.

I have the continued pleasure of observing some of the brightest and most altruistic leaders in the country. In addition to consulting with corporate leaders on strategic planning and consensus-building issues, I frequently work with elected and staff leaders of national not-for-profit associations based primarily in Washington, D.C. The elected and appointed leaders to these national boards of directors are usually at the top of their field, such as leaders in national organizations representing cardiologists, architects, accountants, educators at all levels, and industries such as real estate development, education systems, or marketing. Each leader has attained a high degree of proficiency and respect in his or her field.

Regardless of the profession or industry, many leaders share common traits. However, some exude particular skills and characteristics that were perfect in the situation they were in, thus resulting in powerful leadership and success. Others were in the wrong place at the wrong time, thus ending in an unfortunate conclusion. Alas, here are different leaders for different times and situations.

I hope that learning is the result from these Fly-on-the-Wall observations. To discover strategy and actions that we can apply to our own leadership situations and to teams on which we participate is the ideal outcome. Best wishes for your leadership journey into the familiar and the unknown!

ACKNOWLEDGEMENTS

Here is my opportunity to name those directly involved with helping to accomplish the feat of writing this book, where colleagues and friends are able to deservedly see their name in print, and where the reader gets a glimpse into the author's professional and personal life. Here we go.

To Tom Koerner, editorial director at ScarecrowEducation, my thanks for first inquiring if I would write this book and then providing an informal manner to make the process comfortable and enjoyable.

Thanks to my very early reviewers, for their time, effort and honesty. They include: Scott Eliff who encouraged the writing of an article; Monique Bradbury, a skilled and educated writer; Marilyn Balcombe, a woman of the world with great insights; and Ray Rhinehart, whose words are profound, who always makes me laugh and think, and who tells me about myself sometimes better than I know.

To my second group of reviewers, your input was invaluable in editing and refining: Benny Van Osdell, Lynn Moharam, Beth Weiss, and Janine Pesci, along with professional input from John Moore.

Thanks very, very much to my clients who have given me the joy of working in challenging and exciting situations, and specifically to those whom provided quotes that are included in this book: Cheryl Cummins, Mark Hurwitz, Henry Chamberlain, and Norman Koonce.

To my parents, Bernard and Dorothy Rosenfeld, thank you for being role models of leadership in your own way, which opened doors to my leadership and life pursuits. My father's history as a Lithuanian immigrant, successful businessman, artist, and synagogue leader has created deep roots. My mother's volunteer leadership, cultural arts support, and southern hospitality provide contrasts that add interest and flavor. Thank you for your support and confidence. To sisters Shelley, Tina, and Diane, thank you for listening and encouraging.

Thanks to special friends and extended family who have been supportive in their care and enthusiasm for this book: Beth, Nancy, John, and Mary.

Thanks, Neeko, for going with me to the beach while I wrote, and for providing loving attention.

And most importantly, thanks to Mike and Ryan. Your flexibility, energy, zest for life, devotion, and constancy provide me with a most valuable reminder to stay centered and connected. I love and appreciate you greatly.

You are all appreciated. There are many more who inspired the stories in the following case studies. Thank you for the learning, the challenge, and the opportunity to share with others. I hope from these experiences we all grow to greater wisdom and compassion in our lives.

INTRODUCTION

Dear Leaders,

How many times have you said, "I'd love to be the Fly-on-the-Wall in that situation?"

Well, I am the infamous fly-on-the-wall in boardrooms and management meetings. Rumor has it that you want to talk to me; that you want to see what I see in order to learn. Here is your chance to be the invisible observer. I'm here to share the buzz on leadership as I have viewed it as a consultant to many diverse organizations. I have seen leaders that are good, and leaders that are not so good. Were there recurring themes or patterns that emerged from these observations? Absolutely.

The best of the best leaders included strong demonstrations of genuine commitment, passion, and integrity, as well as effective communication and people skills. The worst of the worst were not only weak in communication style; in some cases they exhibited weak character and questionable behavior. As always, however, personalities either got in the way or helped greatly. Leadership's strengths and weaknesses are revealed in the following pages, along with their effect on strategy, team building, and ultimately, organizational success.

I hope you enjoy this Fly-on-the-Wall perspective to demystify what is really happening in boardrooms and with senior managers. What you will see provides important lessons for leadership opportunities and challenges. Your actions are your legacy. Make each leadership action count.

Fondly yours,
Fly-on-the-Wall

LEADERS MUST PREPARE
FOR THE UNEXPECTED

Leaders learn that unchallenged long-standing relationships can lead to disputes and distrust.

THE ASSIGNMENT

To design and present a business case and proposal requesting funding from a related organization.

WHAT HAPPENED

A national not-for-profit association based in Washington, D.C. started an educational institute in order to provide industry-specific education. After twenty years, the educational institute became stronger financially than the trade association that founded it, with good reserves and growing annual revenues.

In a time of near financial crisis, the association's leadership went to the institute's leadership for a short-term working capital loan. This is like a parent going to an adult child for a loan, after the parent had invested in making the child's business a success. An in-depth financial analysis was prepared by the parent to show the history and anticipated trends of the trade association. A business plan was developed to outline steps for internal reorganization to occur. Additionally, new management of the association represented key staff that had stronger skills and financial savvy than held by previous association staff.

An informal meeting was scheduled for the association's executive director and finance director to present the dire situation to the educational institute's executive. A business case was developed and presented to the leader of the institute, to inform him of a loan request that was coming to his Board of Directors and to obtain his early feedback.

Several hours were spent together in a small conference room at the trade association's headquarters. Questions were asked and answered. Reports were examined and explained. At the conclusion of the meeting, the institute's leader was offered a folder with copies of financial reports. He pushed the folder back to the finance director, declining to take it with no comment other than, "I don't need to take it." He acknowledged the challenging state of affairs and the hard work already in place to improve the status of the trade association. Other general conversation occurred related to the two entities, board members, and activities. After all, this was "family" and an opportunity to catch up with each other. The leaders shook hands and went back to their offices in their respective buildings.

The trade association made the formal request to the educational institute's Board of Directors a few weeks later. The Board of Directors from the institute declined to make the loan to their "parent" organization. Reasons included that they did not receive enough financial information and it appeared to be too risky of a loan venture.

The trade association's leaders were stunned. The finance director thought about the detailed private presentation made earlier and understood now why the institute's executive took no financial papers. The institute's leader could say that not enough information was in his possession. Sadly, the trade association, the parent, that first capitalized this institute twenty years ago and had representatives on the institute's Board of Directors, was rebuffed. The immediate result: a new distant and more volatile relationship with those who were once considered "family" now officially began.

The more competitive and tense nature of the new relationship continued for years. The trade association, under its newly skilled staff and leadership, emerged stronger than ever before, without help from the educational institute. (The trade association ended up borrowing from a bank and making full repayment of the loan within ten months.) The division between the trade association and the educational institute caused strife for leaders. Future struggles worsened. Mediation, one-on-one meetings, letters to association members, and other attempts were made to resolve conflicts. Very little positive was accomplished between the two legally related organizations that operated at more than arms-length apart.

Later, after several years, agreements were made that the two would chart their futures more autonomously and not be constrained by one another. The majority of association members were confused by what the relationship between their trade association and educational institute was. Many industry leaders had loyalties and biases for one or the other organization.

The two entities continue to pursue serving the industry in a combination of integrated and non-integrated agreements. Most efficiencies and joint development opportunities were lost, along with trust and goodwill.

LESSONS LEARNED

- Don't assume previous relationships will be harmonious today, even if the organizations are formally related. Relationships can change quickly.
- Just because you helped an organization in the past does not mean that the group will be there for you in the future.
- Unfortunately, relationships may end in a way that is very different from how they began. Prepare for this from the beginning when you structure and document agreements.
- Every discourse and presentation should be prepared as if it was being presented to outsiders, even when presented to "insiders."
- Always operate in a professional, business-like manner, no matter whom you are working with.

- Maintain thorough documentation of time, place, persons, and content involved in discussions.
- Think competitively and act strategically, at all times. Plan for the unexpected.

To wrap up this case, we need to remember that long-term relationships can reappear in a completely new form no matter if the parties involved are corporations, nonprofits, school board members, or marriage partners. When one party wants or needs something from the other, this affects the dynamics of the relationship and the needs and wants of the other party. Each side will internalize the change in terms of: "How does this affect me? What's my opportunity or risk?"

Trust within a relationship is fragile and can be easily broken, never to be fully regained. Leaders who win think ahead to multiple possible outcomes when actions or decisions are pending. They are prepared to negotiate; they are prepared to withdraw; they are prepared to walk away if necessary. Who you select to collaborate with now may play out in completely different terms in the future. Be prepared.

2

VISION AND TRUST IN COLLABORATIVE LEADERSHIP

Working together with high expectations can result in great accomplishments with trust that has been earned and respected.

THE ASSIGNMENTS

Part 1: To readdress vision priorities
Part 2: To conduct a Leadership Retreat

WHAT HAPPENED

Part I

In the first leadership situation with this large "think tank" type not-for-profit organization, fifty-five board of trustees and fifteen senior staff members came together for one day to reexamine the organization's stated vision, which was related to promoting leadership in improving land use for a better society. Using current internal performance data and industry market conditions, the organization wanted to update priorities that were most necessary to accomplish the long-term vision.

The chief operating officer stated the importance of the vision: "We encompass every sector related to land use. We have to stay focused on the bigger vision in order to fulfill our mission. Otherwise, we could stray off course, given the variety and number of projects and programs we are involved in." Straying off course could have easily happened with this Board of Trustees, all who were very successful entrepreneurs or high-ranking officers in mega-corporations. They were demanding, loved challenges, and importantly, had mutual respect for each other.

Senior staff of the think-tank organization was also entrepreneurial in their approach to serving members and accomplishing the vision. Programs and services were frequently created from scratch to reinvent a new, exciting, and informative experience for these high achieving members. Staff strived for no repetition in design or content of programs. Staff was relentless in delighting members with worthwhile forums and networking opportunities to help members take back valuable learning to their individual companies.

Given the history of the members' successes, delighting them was an enormous challenge. Logistically, members were used to the best accommodations and services in their private lives. From a content perspective, they had heard it all, seen it all, experienced most of it, or invented it.

The staff leaders' persistence, creativity, resourcefulness, and professionalism resulted in a rewarding client/consultant partnership for this assignment. During the visioning engagement, the consultant used cutting-edge technology and strategic thinking designs to take participants on a journey. Top elected leaders of the think tank were kept closely apprised of the approach being planned and were involved with approving the agenda design. They were willing to take a risk in using new technology and new processes because leadership demanded that every experience be worthwhile for participants. Leadership also wanted to offer skill enhancement opportunities so members could contribute to the think-tank organization as future leaders, and also benefit from learning personally and professionally.

The result of the visioning effort was a collaborative success due to focused purpose, agenda planning, and respect for expertise among the elected leaders, staff, consultant, and participants. Leaders who can collaborate to interpret the effect of new influences on their organization and serve as instructive visionaries are winners. They see and understand the big picture. They connect how their mission interacts with the external and internal environment. They have clarity of what the end goal is, yet are open to how the achievement of that goal can proceed. These types of collaborative and visionary leaders are an asset to any company, education system, nonprofit, or government.

Part 2

The second engagement took these successful and, in some cases, powerful leaders on a two-day retreat at a mountain resort to uncover new energy and commitments to themselves for how they can be better leaders within the think-tank organization. Now remember, these are affluent senior executives; they are already proven leaders. Yet, senior staff believed the participants valued more skill development and exchange of experiences to further enlarge their effectiveness with the think tank organization and back home in their own companies.

The trust in staff leadership from these assertive members was strong. Staff worked months with consultants to design the retreat process, with many revisions and discussions, to ensure the experience was most worthwhile for their demanding members. Staff and elected leaders were determined to "get it right" for the participants in the design of the sessions, the choice of speakers, the social settings, and the logistical planning. Nothing was repeated from previous meetings without first examining how it fit into the overall flow and desired outcome from this retreat. Everything was integrated to ensure the experience left the group totally committed to translating the discussions into personal action for improvements to their leadership efforts.

The result was an enlightening weekend for participants, staff, and the consultant. The trust that was present during the design and delivery of the retreat was critical. Acting with integrity, honesty, and respectfulness contributed to the essence of the program's successful outcome. This experience demonstrated many positive attributes of leadership, but maybe most of all, that just when you think leaders appear to know it all, they surprise you with the capability of learning even more about themselves, others, and how to be a more effective leader.

The staff and elected leaders in this organization were inspiring in that they had already succeeded on many fronts, yet they were constantly raising the bar of performance standards. They never rested on their laurels because if they did, their members would not attend, participate, or come back. Their members were constantly being recruited by others to devote their time or money elsewhere, yet they chose this organization as their professional gathering place. Why? Because the caliber of peers was high and the experience was consistently worth their time.

LESSONS LEARNED

- Staff who enjoy the challenge of surprising and delighting a top-notch audience are an asset to behold with great appreciation.
- Collaboration among staff leaders and appointed or elected leaders requires mutual respect and trust.
- Inspiring leaders who have already achieved great things in their lives require a special skill for listening to their wants and desires and delivering with impeccable execution. Working with a group of proven leaders can result in a powerful force for vision, collaboration, and innovation with exceptional accomplishments, as was demonstrated by this organization.

As the author, I take the liberty to wrap up this case with simple encouragement for leaders to demonstrate they value creativity and are willing to take risks in order to achieve great results. Leaders can do this by trusting the person who wants to give "it" (creativity) a try. Whether it is a manager wanting to motivate his staff, or a school principal wanting to encourage her teachers, let them know that taking a risk with a new approach or fresh idea is okay and that you are looking forward to learning from and sharing the results.

LEADERS MUST KNOW WHEN FAVORS MAY NOT BE FAVORS

Leaders lose when a favor turns into unfair advantage, combined with favors that are poorly executed.

THE ASSIGNMENT

To design and facilitate a strategic planning meeting where computer-based tools would aid participants.

WHAT HAPPENED

A critical strategy meeting with the Board of Directors of a national professional society was being conducted. Insights and trends about the profession and the markets it served would be discussed. The facilitator for the session suggested use of special electronic meeting tools that other clients frequently use in strategy-setting meetings. These tools help groups anonymously brainstorm, categorize, vote, and complete other tasks when efficient consensus building is important. Normally, the facilitator coordinated the technical logistics for the special electronic set-up. In this way, the responsibility for the quality of the meeting, both in terms of discussion conclusions and technical support, remained with the facilitator so that accountability could be better controlled for the meeting.

This membership organization had a new staff executive who came from the profession that the association represented. He previously had been active on the Board of Directors, and even an officer at one time. He was deeply committed to the organization and its members, and enjoyed wonderful relationships and friendships from years of involvement.

However, he was quickly learning the "other side" of associations; that of being staff and not a member. New insights were gained as to the demands made on staff, while constantly trying to remain objective and neutral among members. Additionally, making decisions that previously seemed to be straightforward suddenly appeared to be affected by internal politics and, thus, not so clear.

Before providing the specific example this new leader faced, it is necessary to understand the differences in membership classification. A "vendor" or "supplier" member provides products and services to the primary membership group. For example, a doctor's organization would have supplier members who sold medical equipment, uniforms, or office software. Thus, vendors join associations as a marketing and revenue opportunity, and to build relationships with current and prospective customers.

Back to our new staff executive, caught in an unknowingly potential dilemma. When one of the association's vendor members heard that the Board of Directors was using special electronic tools for their upcoming meeting, the vendor offered to host the meeting at his office facility, which happened to have this same electronic set-up in addition to skilled technical staff. The staff executive expressed great appreciation to the vendor member for the generous offer that would save a lot of money in meeting costs, and he accepted the offer. The facilitator was wary, with two primary concerns.

First, the vendor's staff would be present during a Board strategy meeting, and would have early access to key insights and discussions that could provide a competitive advantage to the vendor's company, which other vendor members would not have. The facilitator was con-

cerned that other vendor members of the association might perceive
this access as unfair. This was especially sensitive because each professional member of the association represented potential million dollar
purchase orders to a vendor. If one vendor had early access to competitive data because of a favor, that could cause very delicate problems
with other vendor members.

The nuances of vendor relationships with their customer's associations can be complex. While vendors can buy advertising in the association's magazine or sponsorships of programs for visibility, they are also
considered part of the association's "family" where equality, fairness, and
representation come in to play.

The second concern was that with a "no-cost" offer to use the vendor's
facility and technical staff on a weekend, the facilitator felt that the association must be assured that the meeting logistics and technical support were still of the highest quality, and not delegated to trainees or the
inexperienced. In other words, the facilitator was giving up control of
key ingredients to a successful retreat. The staff executive felt confident
that the meeting would be logistically successful, saying he knew the history of the vendor member and personally had known the contact for
years. His vendor member would deliver a commitment to quality on all
fronts, and he was not concerned that other vendor members may perceive a competitive advantage.

The facilitator still wished to alleviate these concerns further. To help
with the first concern of unfair competitive advantage, the vendor was
requested to sign a confidentiality agreement so that all meeting content
data remained the property of the professional association, and that the
strategic planning process design remained the facilitator's property, and
neither be accessed or used by the vendor.

To help with the second concern of experienced and skilled technical
staff being offered for free, the facilitator sent a separate communication requesting that the vendor's assigned technician respond as soon as
possible to discuss the support requirements for the planning session.
By establishing contact early, the facilitator hoped to ensure everyone
and everything was prepared as needed.

After month-long attempts at contact by the facilitator, with no response, the vendor finally returned the call the week before the meeting.
He signed the confidentiality agreement about content and process with

no comment, and scheduled a meeting the day before the Board of Director's meeting for the facilitator to meet with the technician to review the detailed agenda provided the previous month. The facilitator was used to working with technical support staff weeks in advance, not the day before. But, at least contact with the vendor member was finally completed.

The facilitator arrived at the technical planning meeting at the same location where the Board of Directors would convene the following day. The technician introduced himself and the facilitator asked how many electronic sessions he had supported to date. The response was "zero"! The technician responded to the facilitator's next question that he had never even attended a live electronic meeting, much less provided the required support. Additionally, the technician had never reviewed the detailed agenda, provided weeks in advance to the vendor.

The facilitator was horrified and insisted that the vendor find an experienced technician within the day and call to confirm the person's qualifications. The facilitator had designed a sophisticated and complex meeting agenda based on controlling technical requirements. The staff executive had approved the process, chose to use free vendor support, and did not know about this current dilemma. The facilitator's concern of unqualified support had come true; however, the "show" had to go on to deliver a successful strategy meeting the following day.

The facilitator hunted down experienced technicians to step in for the support role during the next day's meeting, just in case the vendor member could not find qualified and available staff. The facilitator chose not to alarm the association executive about the lack of technical capability for the next day's meeting, especially since the client was in an important Executive Committee meeting at the time. Complaining about his vendor member not providing qualified technical staff would not help the Board meeting the following day.

The vendor finally called that evening to say an experienced technician would be on-site, working with the trainee, who was originally assigned to be there alone. The immediate alarm had subsided, although the normal advance preparation with the technical tools and support staff would be rushed.

During the first day of the two-day Board session, even though great frustration had occurred the previous day, the meeting began smoothly without the client knowing the level of anxiety that had occurred.

Around 1:00 p.m., though, a not-so-funny thing happened. The air conditioning turned off in the high-rise building. The session was scheduled to continue until 4:30 p.m., with much work yet to be accomplished to achieve the goal of the meeting.

The vendor member was immediately informed. After several phone calls, the vendor discovered that the building staff was testing the air conditioner that weekend. Written confirmations from building personnel for logistical requirements related to the Board meeting could not be located. By 3:00 p.m., the computers were hot, as well as the participants, and the session adjourned early, out of necessity. A 7:00 a.m. start for the next day was agreed upon to make up for some of the lost time. The facilitator spent the evening revising the agenda to still be able to accomplish the strategy session's objective by the end of the next day.

When the Board arrived for the early meeting at 7:00 a.m., the doors were locked with no one available to open the building. Finally, over thirty minutes later and with everyone wishing they could have slept longer, the doors were opened. Needless to say, the facilitator was feeling anxious due to the amount of work still to accomplish in less and less time.

At the conclusion of the Board meeting on the second day, a successful result was accomplished. The staff executive thanked the vendor profusely for allowing the use of their fine facility and technical staff. The facilitator was complimented on the process design and assistance in achieving the goals.

The facilitator, however, was not feeling a sense of accomplishment. The frustration with the vendor due to the initial technical crisis, and, later, the shortened meeting time, was unsettling.

The facilitator informed the staff executive about the technical support problem later during a casual private conversation. The staff executive expressed no comment or concern since everything was now under control, technically. He was still pleased with the dollars saved for the meeting facility and electronic support. When problems with the air conditioning and locks caused logistical challenges to accomplishing the meeting's goal, the expectation was that goals could still be achieved. The show must go on, even though the facilitator was not in control of the support requirements and had less time than agreed to for working with the group.

LESSONS LEARNED

- If a situation does not feel ethically or logistically right, go with your gut.
- Talk about your concerns with more than one leader to strive for objective feedback.
- Consider alternatives for the facilitator in this situation, such as (a) insisting on changing the meeting logistics to fit the facilitator's ability to control the technical standards and (b) lowering the bar on the expectations for the deliverable if you no longer have control over support requirements.
- The leader's role in looking at the big picture and listening to possible concerns from internal and external experts is critical. The new staff executive too quickly dismissed any concerns.
- Leaders should at least test concerns for validity before moving forward. In this case, by asking experienced internal staff or leaders from this or other organizations, the leader could ascertain if red flags of warning were problematic.
- This new staff executive may have been too close to the "member view" and not truly objective since he was not a seasoned executive or association manager. New leaders can help themselves and their organizations by realizing the possibility of a lack of clear objectivity when coming from too close to one side of the organization.
- The facilitator could take less responsibility for achieving the meeting goals in this circumstance. In hindsight, calling the client to inform him of the lacking technical support would share responsibility for the meeting's outcome. Additionally, when the meeting time was reduced, discussing expectations and reduced achievement of goals with the staff executive would be appropriate.
- What would you have done as the facilitator in this situation? What would you have done as the staff executive? Do you think it was a good decision to use the vendor's facility, knowing that the perception of unfair competitive advantage may exist among other vendor members? When logistical and technical support fell flat, what would you have done as the executive or facilitator?
- Favors, perceived and real competitive advantages, and expectations for accountability without having decision-making authority

or control, are all issues that leaders must think about when working to achieve goals.

As a wrap-up, it's clear that there are times when professional relationships can get too "cozy" and block objectivity. This is especially
prevalent in small businesses where leaders may be related to staff or
vendors, or even in larger corporations when a leader has a "favored"
subordinate. Looking objectively at the situation and truly listening to
others' warnings or opinions can help the leader win respect for at least
listening, and win trust that a decision was made considering all perspectives.

4

GOOD LEADERSHIP CAN TURN NIGHTMARES INTO DREAMS

A crisis requires using all strengths of all staff, sometimes resulting in co-leadership at the top.

THE ASSIGNMENT

The Chief Financial Officer, along with the Executive Director of an international not-for-profit association, provides co-leadership to turn around a financial and operational crisis.

WHAT HAPPENED

After six months on the job, the Executive Director of this international not-for-profit association was ready to hire a new staff professional to provide a sounder financial infrastructure for the Washington, D.C.-based organization. While there had not been a financial crisis during the executive's early months, he just was not satisfied with the lack of complete answers to his finance-related questions. Too often the finance vice president could not respond and had to go back to staff to do research, with many questions left unanswered. It was time for the finance vice president to leave and for stronger leadership to be brought in.

 Finally, after a broad and intensive search, the right candidate was hired for the position. She was a former banking analyst with strong financial and organizational skills, ready for a new challenge. The executive informed his newly hired Chief Financial Officer (CFO) that he had a feeling what she saw on paper and in financial statements may not tell the whole story, due to the history of lack of sufficient explanations from previous staff. She was given complete authority to examine everything and anything, and to recommend changes in the organization financially and operationally. The CFO would receive the executive's full support visible to staff and elected and volunteer leaders.

The work began immediately. No one could have predicted what the next ten months would bring. The crisis was beyond imagination. Involved were former FBI agents, personnel, insurance companies, attorneys, and many sleepless nights wondering when the nightmare would end.

Week I: Discovery

The new CFO had reviewed financial reports with the executive director prior to accepting the offer of employment. While positive momentum had been made in several areas of the organization, the executive confided that previous financial depth among staff had been insufficient and challenges were expected. He wanted to move forward. He needed to know that he could count on the skills and credibility of his staff leaders.

The CFO considered that the financial reports might lack some integrity and reliability. She noticed there was inconsistent and infrequent documentation to explain financial entries. The lack of organized records was further complicated with vagueness in staff responses to specific questions.

Finally, after a couple of days of digging by the CFO, the red warning flag went up and the bells and lights went off. When talking to the staff person responsible for paying bills, the CFO saw a stack of checks, with invoices attached, about 15 inches high in the locked safe. "What is that?" the CFO asked. "Checks that are waiting to be mailed as soon as we have enough money in the bank to cover them." Gulp. Very bad news.

The CFO immediately met with the executive to explain that while their records showed payments were being made on time for expenses, the prepared checks were, in fact, being held in the safe until funds were available to cover the checks. Then the payments were mailed. The executive sank in his chair. He knew that some suppliers had called regarding late payments, but was not aware of the severity of the situation. He knew cash flow was tight, but not this tight. The executive listened to more news and agreed to alert staff to halt any discretionary expenses and to have operational expenses approved by the CFO until the scope of the cash flow crisis was better understood.

Weeks 2 and 3: Analysis of the Problem(s)

The CFO calculated the dollar amount of checks sitting in the safe, along with projecting other payments that were due over the next few months, in addition to payrolls and rent. The crisis proportion was looming and scary. The executive led the way for the CFO to have full cooperation from all staff, including vice presidents. He demonstrated the seriousness of the matter with his facial expressions and messages. At the same time, he showed great strength in assuring staff that together the problems would be solved and they would emerge stronger than ever before.

The executive director personally escorted the new CFO to meet with each staff vice president in order to quickly learn the operations of the total organization and lines of business.

The executive also called a meeting with the elected officers of the organization. The three officers arrived at the Washington, D.C., headquarters only knowing that large challenges existed and an emergency meeting was necessary. The executive introduced the new CFO and turned the meeting over to her for the presentation. There was grave silence following the presentation. The officers were shocked to discover that if dramatic changes were not immediately made, the organization would end the year with a $300,000 deficit. The organization did not have the necessary level of reserves to cover such a deficit. The officers learned that prepaid dues for the following year from members had been used to cover cash flow needs in the current year. Therefore, the organization quickly ran out of money when needed in the new year, because it had already been spent to pay for last year's expenses.

Further, the financial records in the past did not reflect the magnitude of problems due to how financial entries were made. The place had endured sloppy financial and operational controls, and now the organization was revealing the result of such poor management.

Unfortunately, this was just the tip of the iceberg. The real drama was about to begin.

Weeks 4, 5, and 6: Working Through the Mess

Daily, the CFO reviewed disbursements and worked out arrangements for payments with vendors. The staff was scared about their jobs and the future of the organization, but they numbly proceeded with hopeful faith that the new CFO and the executive would lead them out of the problems. Calm reassurance was provided: stay the course, we'll figure it out, we're a team, we can do it – all messages repeated frequently by the executive.

Senior staff met for long hours to cut expenses and pursue new sources of revenue. The accounting staff was reorganized, with the manager dismissed for incompetence in fulfilling duties to maintain records according to accepted accounting principles. New, higher-skill staff was recruited. The backlog of work in financial reconciliation to bank records was daunting. At the same time, staff had to begin a new budgeting process for the upcoming fiscal year. They were to follow a new business plan approach recommended by the CFO and supported by the executive. Daily formal and informal discussions addressed financial crisis, staff concerns, incompetence, and plans for the future. It was a nightmare at the workplace.

About this time, the executive and CFO reached a turning point in their relationship, as co-leaders in the turnaround. They each brought skills and strengths. While the CFO was the numbers and analytical expert, working behind the scenes and in front view scouring the organization's finances and operations, she was only leading the technical aspect of the turnaround. Yes, that was important, but it would not accomplish the turnaround alone.

The executive director was the chief morale booster. His natural and instinctive ability to rally the staff with his informal style, good humor, and surprise treats kept the staff focused to get through the dirty work of a turnaround. He made the job fun when it normally would not be fun. Staff worked long hours. They stayed even though they were scared their jobs would be lost. Informal pizza parties, ice cream truck visits, and one-on-one conversations with the executive began the threads that bound a team together.

His passion was contagious. He was mobilizing staff to excel no matter what the circumstances. He showed caring for the staff and maintained an optimistic spirit for the elected leaders. The executive commented, "Enthusiasm is contagious and is a fundamental element of leadership. If the leader does not fully embrace the organization's mission with passion, energy, and commitment, the team will not reach its full potential."

The bond was forming among staff, although not recognized at that time. Other senior staff began to "take care" of his or her employees by being more accessible to talk, quickly rewarding anything good that happened, and participating in all organizational informal gatherings. But the strength of the threads was about to be tested.

Week 7: The Crisis Hits Its Peak

An employee had resigned about a month earlier, after the CFO's first week on the job. The employee stated she was pursuing other opportunities; a good-bye party was held and she was wished well. Now, at week seven of the crisis, her attorney called to inform the executive director that the employee was admitting to embezzlement of approximately $55,000 over several years. She wanted to "come clean" voluntarily and cooperate. The executive and CFO would never know if she came forward because she thought she would eventually be caught through the turnaround that was underway, or because of her desire for personal redemption. Most likely, it was the former because admissions of guilt and cooperation are usually given in hope of lesser charges and punishment. The work of thorough discovery, however, was only beginning.

The executive and CFO quickly contacted attorneys, auditors, and the insurance company carrying their Employee Dishonesty coverage. The elected officers were informed. The locks on the building were changed. Key codes in the computer system were changed.

Staff was in shock. The guilty employee had been a star team player for years, moving up quickly in responsibility. Her duties involved interaction with accounting functions, mail functions, inventory, and office, management. The CFO traced the employee's many functions and interactions and developed lists of questions to communicate between attorneys to obtain more information. The Employee Dishonesty coverage had recently been increased from $50,000 to $200,000, only months earlier by the previous finance director after an insurance review, providing the only feeling of some relief.

The executive was in a difficult situation. The elected officers were angry and suspicious that others could be involved with the embezzlement. Everyone on staff, except the new CFO, could be "suspect" for wrongdoing in the officers' eyes. They wanted answers about how this could happen. The tension was rising.

The executive and CFO talked daily with attorneys. Brainstorming angles for how the embezzlement happened, how much money was really stolen, and who was involved, all gave the aura of a surreal detective story.

Meanwhile, the cash flow was still in crisis, daily calls to vendors occurred to delay payments, management of staff fears was required, in addition to recruiting new accounting staff, and next year's budget development. Leadership and staff were looking to each other for support. The executive consistently played the role of "chief cheerleader" while the staff needed that relief. Even if they sometimes questioned the authenticity of his messages, the morale boost and humor avoided a downward spiral of fear and inaction.

WEEK 8: PLAYING DETECTIVE

The executive was away on travel during week eight, leaving the CFO in charge related to the embezzlement. As the sole liaison to attorneys, auditors, insurers, and officers, that was no small task. Conference calls with attorneys were held to uncover the method of embezzlement. Specific "yes" and "no" questions were drafted to ask the guilty employee, through legal counsel. A private detective was brought into the case to identify if collusion with other individuals had occurred.

The method of embezzlement began with the former employee receiving all mail as office manager. Normally, a mail clerk would sort mail. For the past few years, internal controls were extremely weak.

Checks in envelopes would sometimes be routed to departments other than accounting. The number of checks received in a day was not logged in. Serving as office manager, the guilty employee would sometimes sort out checks for book purchases, when customers' checks were written to the organization only using its initials. Since inventory of books and products was not regularly counted, she would remove items from inventory purchased with the checks she had stolen. Since postage was not monitored, the guilty employee would pack and ship the books to the customer, thus promptly serving a happy customer, and helping the mail staff, the inventory staff, and the packaging staff with their work.

However, she had opened a bank account with the same initials as the organization's and was depositing these checks for personal use. She did this for four years.

The bank was negligent in allowing her to open the account without proper corporate papers. They cooperated fully and provided copies of bank statements. Meanwhile, a polygraph test on the guilty employee was arranged to try to obtain further information. The CFO rode in the car to the detective's office with the organization's attorney, who had just received the bank statements. In the car, the CFO began adding up the deposits over the last four years made by the employee to her illegal business account. The total was not $55,000. It was over $100,000.

Financial and technical questions were provided to the detective to ask the former employee. Emotional outbursts, drama, and unbelievable stories of how the employee felt she was brainwashed by a boyfriend, what they spent the money on, and other details were revealed. It was a memorable experience for the CFO, but not one to be repeated.

The CFO had been keeping the executive informed every day while he was away. The officers were also updated regularly. The staff were curious and received non-confidential information. Regular communication was critical.

Upon learning the details of the embezzlement method, the CFO recommended that the audit firm for the organization be fired. Even though these auditors had brought up problem issues in the past related to dividing duties so one person did not have too much access for wrongdoing, recent audit reports did not mention this as a current problem. Audit reports lacked follow-up that past problems had not been corrected, with the problems omitted from reports. A new auditing firm was brought in to conduct an Internal Control Study to finally put weaknesses in full view, along with what had already been discovered. This was the end of the first two months on the job for the CFO.

Months 3 through 6: Progress

It was now Labor Day. The events from Labor Day to December proved to be equally as frustrating as the previous two months; however, startling changes were beginning to occur. The executive collaborated with his senior staff to take a harsh look at human resources. They examined what skills and attitudes were needed. The result was that over the next several months, staff turnover would reach 70%.

Some staff was asked to leave through reorganization and assignments, and others chose to leave with the new emphasis on responsibility and accountability. As new hires were recruited, enhanced skills were brought in. The slow learning curve, as a result of little documentation, frustrated all departments. However, the improved ideas and new methods evolved to make the organization much stronger.

The executive made a special point of integrating the new team of employees with the old team. He wanted to ensure that the old team didn't feel that they were "incompetents" contributing to the downfalls of the past. He didn't want them to feel threatened with fear of losing their jobs by these new higher skilled professionals. Instead, he emphasized that they were the survivors. They had helped the organization weather a terrible storm and should feel proud of their accomplishments.

At the same time, he had a new team of more skilled employees who didn't have the same bond as the old team, yet they wanted to come in and make a difference. It was a delicate balance of not letting the old team feel trodden on, yet ensuring that the new team respected the pains the old team had just experienced.

It took time for the teams to merge into one. There were some struggles. Newer employees sometimes complained of lack of resources or technology, only to be told by old employees how lucky they were to have what they did. Existing employees brought up the past frequently, to finally be told by new employees, "enough already with the past!"

Over time, and with new accomplishments involving this newly integrated team, a new bond was formed between the two different groups.

Meanwhile, the executive and CFO were still managing the turnaround as co-leaders. The daily cash flow was scrutinized with better projections for needs, and early warnings for challenges. A new accounting manager was hired from the banking industry, and she prioritized tasks, trained staff, and managed the "clean up" of accounting records. The special Internal Control Study was completed with a confirmation of serious lack of internal controls and recommendations for immediate action. The initial projection for a year-end deficit of $300,000 was down to a projected $30,000 deficit. This was accomplished by programs being halted, vacant positions not being filled, and expenditures being closely monitored.

An Employee Dishonesty insurance claim recovered over $100,000 in stolen funds, after numerous hours of investigation. Senior staff implemented a new budget and planning process. Other financial controls were put into place. And finally, the executive and CFO went as a team to banking officials to obtain a working capital line of credit. Through their combined credentials along with those of new staff, a solid business plan, and commitment to the future success of the organization, they were approved for a $350,000 unsecured line of credit, despite the organization's unfavorable financial history. The news was shared with staff and all celebrated a feeling of having reached a turning point.

In preparation for a Board meeting and other governance meetings scheduled for early December, communications were distributed to a broader section of leaders of the organization during this time, through written materials and audiocassettes. Volunteer leaders were assured that a full presentation would occur with plenty of time for questions.

At the December meeting, the volunteer leaders went through a catharsis. During this face-to-face meeting, three hundred volunteer leaders vocalized their anger and frustration. The comments were not necessarily directed at the new staff who had inherited the problems, yet it was painful for all to endure. The meetings ended with some skepticism and a requirement that staff would have to prove itself every step of the way during this turnaround. The new budget was cut and aggressive income targets were set.

Months 7 through 10: Accomplishments

The executive director took the charge from elected and volunteer leaders seriously. His energy and focus provided a role model to other staff. His enthusiasm permeated throughout the organization. He continued to recognize staff efforts regularly and reward achievements through formal and informal means. The staff accepted the challenge and was determined to succeed.

The accomplishments were beginning to come more regularly now. The year-end audit letter from new auditors included a glowing report of improvements to internal controls. Diligence, commitment, and proper guidance were commended. Marketing sales goals were exceeded due to more effective planning, supervision, and incentives. Significant improvements in cash management enabled the line of credit to be repaid earlier than expected. Short-term investments exceeded targets, resulting in higher interest earnings. Other financial controls and improvements in operations were recognized. Through the co-leadership of the executive and CFO, tangible and dramatic improvements in cost controls, accountability, and planning were achieved. With the talents of new staff, new ideas and methods were accomplished with success.

The Turnaround is Completed

The final measure of achievement occurred during the organization's annual convention in June, attended by more than two thousand people. The outpouring of verbal and written support, compliments, praise, confidence, encouragement, and enthusiasm were astounding. The members of the organization were excited and ready to move forward. The staff felt their support. The executive was proud of his staff and what had been accomplished. He shared the recognition often and throughout the staff. "Stand aside and shine the light on others" was his frequent remark. Confidence had been re-gained. The turnaround was complete.

LESSONS LEARNED

- Listen to your gut instinct if responses to questions do not make sense or are unclear. Dig further to get questions answered satisfactorily.

- In times of crisis, the need for regular communication is more critical than ever.
- Know your strengths. Identify what traits and skills are most needed for leading specific situations. If you don't have everything that is needed, join forces to collaborate as a leadership team.
- Expose your passion and commitment; it's contagious.
- Tell the truth all the time. Credibility, especially during a turn-around, is critical.
- Think about who is on your team—the personalities, the history together, the different motivators for different people. Respect the needs of the individuals to make a whole team.
- Give others credit for ideas and accomplishments to contribute to high performance feedback. "Stand aside and shine the light on others."

This situation could happen in any type of profit, nonprofit, or municipal organization. Planned and honest communications are so critical. Depending upon the type of entity, you may have a town hall meeting for a school district or large employer. You may have mass mailings to corporate investors. And when constituents have a catharsis and begin to point fingers of blame, it is important to stand tall, respond professionally, and acknowledge the concerns.

When the budget was cut, after all the hard work already underway, the executive did not act like a victim. His determination to rise to the challenge motivated staff. Leaders can make or break the outcome by their reaction to challenges.

Co-leadership requires working as a team and keeping egos in check. In corporate situations, you sometimes find someone from Marketing or Finance or Technology all of a sudden promoted to the number two slot of leadership. There is usually a void to fill at the top with a critical need for emphasis in a specific area. Or, the personality of the co-leader is needed to balance out the chief executive's style.

This was a case with much pain at the time, but great learning afterwards.

5

LEADERS ARE PEOPLE TOO—THEY HAVE IMPERFECTIONS

The cause of an outburst or reaction may have nothing to do with the issue at hand. Anyone can have a bad day.

THE ASSIGNMENT

To design and conduct a comprehensive electronic survey for use on-site at the annual convention of a national association.

WHAT HAPPENED

As part of its strategic planning process, this national association desired to assess the performance of many different aspects of the association. A bank of computers was installed at the convention with an online multi-page survey available for members to take during certain hours of the convention. Members could complete the survey in approximately fifteen to twenty minutes. Following the convention, the leaders of the association wanted to have summary results for use at various committee meetings that were to occur at the conclusion of the convention.

The survey consultant helped the association prepare an in-depth promotional plan to gain survey participation among the convention attendees. Announcements to members about the important survey were released prior to the convention through email and postcards, and also from the podium during general sessions at the convention. Extensive signage was placed around the meeting facility to remind members to take the survey. Incentives and gifts were provided upon completion of the survey instrument. Buttons and stickers were given to encourage others to ask about the survey. A reminder notice was printed in the convention program.

A Challenge to achieving high survey participation during the convention was quickly recognized upon arrival at the facility. The room location assigned for the bank of survey computers was not in the mainstream of traffic and required an out-of-the-way walk by attendees. New signs were made on-site to give directions, add more color, and to grab attention. Additionally, staff at the registration desk was encouraged to "talk up" the importance of the survey to members when they registered or came by to ask questions.

At the conclusion of the convention, the survey data was tabulated. The data produced insights into the preferences and thinking of members, with profiles and demographics instantly recorded. However, the results reflected lower than expected number of survey participants. The goal was to strive for a 200–300 person participation rate, but only 150 surveys were completed. While the information may not be scientifically or statistically representative, there was no doubt that a wealth of insights was collected that could be further explored.

Meanwhile, the elected president of the association, himself a long-standing member, was excited to be leading the organization during the time of strategic planning. He maintained his professional career (his paying job) in senior management at a very large organization, while enjoying the role as president of his national association immensely. This leadership position gave him opportunities with peers, suppliers, and the general industry that he otherwise would not have had.

A few weeks earlier, he had expressed some concern about what he would do when his term as elected president was over, especially since he was in an unstable situation at his workplace. Understandably, his emotions were somewhat uneven as his year in office was winding down.

However, with the strategic planning process in full throttle and the annual convention looming ahead, he was focusing on the important work and high visibility still remaining during his term as president.

After the convention concluded, the association's staff director and elected president met with the survey consultant to review the results. During this debriefing meeting at the convention hotel, the elected president was visibly disappointed with the lower than expected participation in the survey. The promotional efforts and extra visibility provided on-site were reviewed. The poor location to take the survey was deemed the primary contributor to low turnout, along with excellent speakers and networking that competed for the time and attention of participants. Additionally, the extensive nature of the survey did require a time commitment from participants of approximately fifteen to twenty minutes.

There was a pause in the conversation after the review of summary results was completed. The president went to the mini-bar for a beverage, and surprisingly, came back with a beer. Traditionally, drinking alcohol in the afternoon during business meetings was uncharacteristic in the association. Watching the president's irritable behavior quickly progress, the consultant presumed that this was probably not the first drink of the day for him.

The president's voice became louder and his dissatisfaction grew stronger. The staff director said nothing to support the promotional effort that had been made or the usefulness of the survey results. Agitation and frustration were clearly present in the room. Finally, the volatile situation ended with an agreement for how to present the detailed survey report, in terms of sorting and profiling. The meeting ended abruptly. The elected president quickly left the room, and the association director silently departed also. It was a confusing and frustrating moment for those involved with the hard work of the survey and convention.

LESSONS LEARNED

- Sometimes things are outside of our control, whether we are working with leaders or anyone else.

- Leaders are people too; they have imperfections and bad days.
- There may be actions that appear to be one thing on the surface, only to be revealed later as something entirely different. The cause of an outburst or passionate argument may have nothing to do with the topic at hand. The originating source of others' feelings can be such a mystery to those who don't know each other well. The president's outburst in the case above was most likely not totally related to the low survey participation levels. His desire to conclude his term in office on a high note of achievement resulted in an outburst of frustration when things didn't appear to be going his way. Who knows what else was going wrong for him that day?
- The good news is that most leaders have attained a level of familiarity in being in the spotlight to understand the importance of not being volatile with emotions or frustrations.
- Remember to not take others' emotional baggage personally. Maintain a professional demeanor at all times and do the best you can with what you know.
- When nominating or placing someone in a leadership position, be alert to warnings of volatile personality streaks, sudden outbursts, or impulsive behavior.
- Ask a candidate how he or she operates under times of high stress. Also, ask the same question to others whom have worked with this prospective leader.
- Ultimately, leaders must be collaborators and must be able to retain respect from those around him or her. A cool head and a steady hand are necessary to steer the ship forward.

I don't think that much more needs to be said by way of a wrap-up with this case. When you are dealing with any human being, personality and emotions are part of the package. Stay objective and look at the situation from all perspectives.

6

LEADERS GIVE STAFF WINGS TO FLY

Leaders that turn staff loose to take risks can generate great ideas and results.

THE ASSIGNMENT

To design and facilitate a planning retreat for a marketing firm that wanted to set priority goals and create action plans.

WHAT HAPPENED

The founder and chairman of this marketing company wanted to use the valuable insights of her professional staff in a planning session to set priority goals for the next two years. The fifteen senior employees were mostly under the age of thirty-five and most had not been involved in strategic planning previously. In addition to the chairman's desire for staff involvement, the president of the company was looking for more buy-in, creativity, and ownership of goals by the staff that primarily reported to the president. During the introductory planning meeting for the retreat with the facilitator, the staff was spirited, appreciative, and excited about the opportunity to help create the future of the company.

Finally, the weekend arrived. At the planning retreat, the chairman remained mostly quiet and let the staff freely explore ideas without her influence. Likewise, the president also watched the creativity at work and interjected ideas only when necessary to help keep the focus of company objectives in the forefront of discussions.

The session was refreshing and exciting for all involved. Politics, territories, and egos were at a minimum. The desire to "really make a difference" in the industry and in the company was at a maximum. The participants' commitment to find viable solutions to challenges was demonstrated by their intensity and unwillingness to give up or just settle for easy answers.

Leadership's commitment and faith in the staff and in implementing the ideas from the retreat were evident. There was a "turning loose" of control by leadership that could have been viewed as risky and not genuine. Senior officers opened the doors for creativity and breakthrough collaboration to see what result could be generated. There was no turning back after the doors were opened.

The reins of the company were offered to professional staff during the planning process to see where they would go. It was creative, inspiring, and motivating. The ownership of the plans, the commitment to help each other, and the desire to see the company excel were all outcomes to make leadership proud.

LESSONS LEARNED

- Refreshing creativity and team spirit are strong assets to nurture and encourage.
- Creativity is frequently assumed with marketing professionals. However, even greater creative synergy will result when a mix of staff is teamed in a new way with a new purpose.
- Youthful spirit of staff can be a great asset with "out-of-the-box" thinking. Thinking as a child might think frequently takes you to the root cause of the problem and aids in responding with the best solution.

- Hiring and training a young team requires patience and skill and constant development.
- The willingness of leadership to not try to control every idea or activity if they want commitment to action was critically important.
- Harnessing spirit, talent, and commitment can result in powerful models of success, especially when constructive collaboration is a cornerstone of a company's culture.

Enabling creativity requires taking risks and giving up some control. If leaders want breakthrough strategies and amazing performance, they have to be willing to nurture the atmosphere to let creativity happen. This could occur with new product development, fabulous customer service, or new methods for teaching children: all requiring an element of risk-taking and a staff with the desire to excel.

7

DON'T LET ONE VOICE ZAP PROGRESS: LEADERS, SPEAK UP!

Leaders excel when they are team players and can build consensus.

THE ASSIGNMENT

According to the client, the assignment was to analyze internal staff and operational structures for congruency with the organization's mission and long-term goals. Some members of the Executive Committee, however, had other ideas as to the purpose of the assignment.

WHAT HAPPENED

The executive director of the national organization approved the scope of services for a consulting engagement after a thorough discussion was completed about his organization's needs. The areas to be reviewed by the consultant were confirmed, as were the scope of recommendations he desired. It is important to note that the executive director specifically did not want the governance structure included in the scope of the study, even when pressed by the consultant about the importance of committees, Boards, and decision-making authority in accomplishing the organization's mission and goals. The executive director responded that this assignment was at the direction of his Executive Committee not to expand into governance structures and issues. Therefore, even though the integration of governance in accomplishing the mission is critical, he reiterated that only the internal operations and staff were to be addressed, thereby focusing more on tactical resources.

After a lengthy process of staff interviews and analyses of processes and operations, the consultant drafted the report. The executive director accepted a final version of the report and distributed it to his Executive Committee. A conference call with the Executive Committee and consultant was scheduled.

During the conference call discussion, a question popped up about the scope of the study. While there were no major concerns about the internal structural recommendations, one Executive Committee member repeatedly dominated the discussion with his disappointment that the governance structure was not addressed in the report. After awhile, when no one spoke up to support the comment or agreed-upon scope of the study, the consultant responded that governance was specifically not requested within the scope of services.

The executive director did not expand to support the consultant's words, nor did he offer any further explanation. Meanwhile, the consultant was sitting face-to-face in front of the executive director during the conference call wondering what was going on with such lack of assertiveness by leadership.

Finally, one other member of the Executive Committee mentioned that he thought they had discussed governance's role within the study, and agreed not to include it. The other members of the Executive Committee said nothing in reference to their recall of the approved scope of the study. Additionally, in their silence, they did not echo agreement with the one member who felt governance was supposed to be included in the report. Thus, the remaining Executive Committee members offered no counter to their outspoken peer who chose to ignore previous consensus decisions made by the group. Likewise, they offered no support as to accurate recollections of agreements made.

It was a state of avoidance with no debate, yet also no agreement with no other voices on either side offered, except for the original two comments from the executive committee members.

The call ended with discussion that the report was helpful and would be reviewed in further detail for implementation. However, an overall melancholy mood was apparent among participants given that a comprehensive study that they had commissioned and which cost a material amount, had just been delivered. Instead of celebration in accomplishing a goal of internal review, they were deflated by the ire of the dominant voice and the lack of consensus support. There was obvious dissatisfaction by the one committee member related to governance, and there was dissatisfaction by the other members related to the fact that no one spoke up to confront the accuracy of the facts.

Immediately following the conference call, back in the executive director's office, he explained to the consultant that the particular dissenting person had initially requested that governance be included in the study, but that the Executive Committee had approved the final scope, without governance, in a majority vote. Even though the vote was final and the contract was signed for scope of services, and the work completed as directed, the member still chose to bring up his dissatisfaction with the omission of governance in the report.

LESSONS LEARNED

- Some people are unable to be team players or live by consensus decisions. If they do not get their own way, they will make life miserable for everyone else by reminding others of the issue on a regular basis. They frequently are unable to support the group's majority decision when it differs from their opinion. While they may have valuable perspectives to share, these people should be carefully guided to roles in the organization that do not stall decision-making or impair unified implementation of decisions.

- Peers on a Board of Directors or Executive Committee will often choose not to overtly challenge or confront a colleague on their own Board. Instead, they frequently choose an outsider to get the heat or punishment, whether that is staff, contractors, or others. Board members often do not want to upset the apple cart within their own group unless it is a life-or-death situation for the organization. They also may not want to risk personal or professional relationships when the confrontation will lead to disagreements with passionate, influential, or domineering peers within the Board. This is when leadership is not working.

- Create a safe environment in the very beginning for equal sharing of viewpoints in a professional and constructive manner. Outline ground rules and responsibilities for consensus decision-making so that respect and productivity can occur.

- Consider the use of an experienced facilitator when dominant personalities get in the way of progress. Support the facilitator in dealing with conflict resolution.

- Be very clear with the group that all opinions are welcome and that respect for differences of opinion is a must. Likewise, define "consensus" for the group, such as the will of the majority after inclusive discussion, with an expectation for the total group to support the decision and speak with one voice.

- Prepare in advance for volatile moments by speaking to multiple respected leaders early in the decision-making process. Encourage them to speak up to share their perspectives no matter how much or how little they may differ with someone else.

- Remind all leaders that it is their responsibility to speak up and to represent the well-being of the whole organization. That is how they can be of most value as a leader to their constituents.

There are many public and private Boards, commissions, and work groups where this applies. There are political reasons, personal reasons, extrovert vs. introvert reasons, and communication style reasons for why a person chooses to speak up or not. When serving in a leadership capacity where you are representing a constituency, it is the responsibility of the leader to put excuses aside and focus on the the best interests of the organization.

8

THE LEADER IS FIRED: NOW WHAT?

A delicate balancing act ensues when the leader who hired you is
fired.

ASSIGNMENT

To design and facilitate a transformational strategic planning process
for a large not-for-profit organization based in Washington, D.C.

WHAT HAPPENED

Note: This case study could apply to a hired consultant or a hired employee.

A gregarious and visionary chief executive of a national organization inspired his chairman and Board of Directors to move forward with a comprehensive strategic planning process. After all, that was one of the reasons
he was hired within the past year—to identify and implement major new
changes for the organization. He interviewed consultants for the important
planning work that needed to be completed and made a recommendation
for whom to select, which was accepted and approved by the Board.

The intensive planning process was initiated. The chief executive arranged for the consultant to be introduced to the Board at its next meeting. The consultant made a presentation highlighting the steps in the planning process about to be undertaken. Support from the Chairman and Board members was confirmed. They were eager to begin.

Staff, leaders, and the consultant were busy with planning tasks from the very beginning. Data was collected, informational meetings were held, and periodic communications were distributed to members and leaders.

About two months after the start of the planning process, another regularly scheduled Board of Directors meeting was held. Immediately following the Board Meeting, the planning consultant was to work with the chief executive and his senior staff on some operational priorities. Several hours into the senior staff meeting, discussions became vague related to collaborative efforts between senior staff and the Board, and the future outlook of relations among leaders and staff. It was a very confusing moment, especially for the consultant, because everyone stopped talking. The senior staff looked at each other or did not make eye contact at all. The chief executive sat silent. What was going on? No one wanted to raise the scary and possibly ugly truth: The Board and the chief executive were not getting along.

The planning consultant, who was trying to facilitate discussion, finally coaxed the senior staff into talking. It felt like a family therapy session! It was grueling and painful at first. One person had to be courageous and start talking. After the planning consultant pulled a chair into the middle of the small group, she silently stared back at the senior staff. A vice president finally broke the ice and explained to the consultant what had happened, quickly putting the truth on the table for all to acknowledge.

At the Board meeting that had just finished, an executive session had been called by the officers. A decision was made to put the chief executive on notice because some things needed to change in terms of his personal style of leadership and communication. The conflict appeared to be about a difference in human chemistry and style, possibly some egos, and the perceived control of the organization. Since this organization spoke to legislators, the media, and related not-for-profits on behalf of a large membership body, the person at the top received high visibility. The Executive Committee of the Board recommended to the full Board that the chief staff executive be placed on "notice" related to the continuation of his employment.

The reasons for the probationary period were not clear to the consultant, nor specified at the senior staff meeting. The chief executive did no financial wrongdoing. The performance of the organization appeared on track to improvement during the executive's short tenure, with several new important hires completed, including vice presidents and consultants.

Finally, the discussion during the senior staff meeting became fully engaged, constructive, and optimistic. Fortunately, the facilitating consultant had worked with the chief executive previously and knew he was a person relatively comfortable in sharing his feelings and listening to others share their feelings. He could handle the candor; he knew he had to work with the team.

By the end of the meeting, the senior staff was determined to rally their support as a senior team, to reassure other staff that they were together in moving forward with plans and improvements, and that they supported the chief executive. They wanted to deflect rumors and assure staff of the constancy of the staff leadership team. A brief communication was carefully crafted and distributed to staff soon thereafter, since the news was already out that the recent Board meeting had been uncomfortable and uncertain as to the future of the chief executive.

During the following two months, there was frequent dialogue internally among staff as to the uncertainty of staff leadership's future. Any program or initiative begun by the chief executive was somewhat uncertain as to its future. The very important and highly visible and endorsed strategic planning process was also affected because the chief executive had hired the consultant. However, much of what the chief executive had started, and the new employees and consultants he had brought in, were lauded as successes by the Board.

The planning consultant stayed focused on the strategic planning process and carrying out the tasks agreed upon. One of the new vice presidents hired by the executive also stayed focused and delivered results that pleased the Board. However, it was an awkward time for all.

The chief executive continued his role and his work, but the tension and uncertainty caused strain as the staff, Board, and executive awaited any final decisions about the continuation of his employment.

Meanwhile the strategic planning process continued and received very high visibility within the organization. The importance of the recommendations from planning would shape the national membership organization for years to come. The planning team, who were members of the organization, worked hard over many months to strategize major objectives that would transform the organization.

The planning consultant was periodically alerted to updates about the executive's status. It was important to know what was going on in the background while the planning work was evolving. What they were building within the strategic plan would be a legacy to work from for the organization over the next few years. How would the plan be accepted knowing that the chief executive had hired the planning consultant and had helped to select the planning team?

The planning consultant and several others hired by the chief executive were firm in their unwillingness to enter into debate or discussion related to the merits or concerns of the chief executive. The focus was on the work to be done. The performance demonstrated by those hired by the chief executive would speak louder than any words. The Executive Committee watched, naturally concerned about "loyalties" from those who were brought in by the chief executive. The focus, however, from those being watched continued to be on their responsibilities and not on the politics or side conversations.

Finally, the decision was made. The chief executive was asked to resign. Now what would happen to the strategic planning process, the new hires, and the programs launched by the chief executive?

For the most part, performance was measured and rewarded appropriately. The strategic planning process was allowed to be completed; it even received applause by the Board upon adoption. The planning consultant did not have interference, and the plan continues to guide the organization even after several years of completion. The vice president hired by the chief executive was later promoted to a more senior staff position due to demonstration of positive results. There was a shake out of non-performing programs, consultants, and staff, but that is to be expected during a turnover. And the chief executive later found a new executive position elsewhere where his style and manner were appreciated and valued. Thus, a very tense and potentially hostile situation had a relatively happy ending after more than one year of painful struggles.

LESSONS LEARNED

- When the "chemistry" of personality and style clash between leaders, it is very difficult to overcome that obstacle. When one has more authority over the other, the person with less authority frequently will lose no matter what their performance or support systems may say.
- Stay out of the fray. Don't engage in discussion or debate when a philosophical difference in style, ego, or control is at stake. Rational arguments frequently are discounted and, instead, emotions enter into the picture.
- Treat all parties with respect and courtesy. You never know who is going to be in charge next.
- If you think you are at risk in relation to such internal battles, prove yourself with competency and integrity. Demonstrate your value with performance and enthusiasm.
- Be aware of the chatter in the background, but don't let it interfere with the job to be done.
- Defer to others' authority. If someone has the power to make decisions or strongly influence decisions, respect that authority.
- Show compassion to other staff. This is a time of uncertainty, mixed emotions, fear of losing jobs, and change. Give someone the benefit of the doubt.
- This is a time to be present, but not overly critical. Again, listen, but stay focused on what your responsibilities and span of control are.
- Finally, don't underestimate the importance of personal style and the potential for clashes with those in charge. Know your style, know your colleagues and bosses' style, and make every effort to be flexible to accommodate others.

As with other cases related to personality of leaders, this case could happen in any type of private or public entity. Knowing that the person who hired you may one day be removed from his or her position opens the door to how important it is to work well with many others and focus on the job and not just pleasing one person.

LEADERSHIP LISTENS AND TAKES ACTION

Leaders who listen to challenging feedback and who include all stakeholders in strategic planning become winners.

THE ASSIGNMENT

To design and facilitate a transformational strategic planning process for a national organization based in Washington, D.C.

The assignment included extensive data collection from multiple stakeholders of the large organization. Several task force meetings occurred to absorb the stakeholder input and to deliberate upon the recommended course of action. Drafts of new organizational concepts and issues learned from the data were distributed to key members and leadership groups to keep them up to date in the strategy development process. Finally after several rounds of feedback sessions, specific goals and objectives were recommended to the Board of Directors for long-term action for the organization.

WHAT HAPPENED

This professional organization is well respected in the not-for-profit industry due to its size, visibility, and success. Its members are intelligent, creative, and demanding, in both their professional and volunteer lives. The organization's staff works closely with elected and volunteer leaders to strive to satisfy many priorities. This fragmentation sometimes causes difficulties when multiple directions dilute the focus and effectiveness of the overall entity.

A comprehensive "vision" for the organization had been developed ten years previously; however, the link from that vision to current actions and priorities was weak. While current goals and policies existed, an overall strategic long-range plan was lacking in the organization thus preventing it from moving forward with consensus to a clear future destination.

There was a desire among many leaders to pull the organization into the next century by questioning some basic traditions and assumptions of who qualifies for membership and what services should be offered. There was a large market share of qualified professionals who had chosen *not* to belong to the organization. Why? Other not-for-profit professional societies were popping up and capturing a share of that market. What could leadership do to welcome greater diversity in membership and strengthen the value of services offered?

Additionally, some members were concerned about their ability to compete in new markets with new competitors. Did members have the right skills to compete? Were there important trends or patterns that members and the organization were ignoring? All of these questions needed to be addressed.

After much preparation with the organization's staff executive about the design and goals of the planning process, the consultant worked with elected officers and senior staff to carefully construct the ideal strategic planning task force. It was important to ensure that a diverse, representative, and knowledgeable task force was appointed. Officers were willing to depart from tradition by including not only current leaders on the task force, but also younger future leaders, outside experts, and a mayor interested in the affect of the profession on public communities. Sufficient resources were approved and allocated for an internal staff liaison to support the planning effort, along with resources for retreats and meetings, data collection, and professional consulting services.

The perceived importance for being selected to serve on the task force was very high. Appointees were committed and willing to put controversial issues on the table for deliberation. Senior elected leaders and staff stayed out of the way of the task force's work, supporting the effort as requested, and publicly valuing and communicating the importance of the strategic planning process. An overview of the planning process approved by the organization's leaders follows.

Comprehensive research was conducted to ensure that a wide range of perspectives was included. This inclusive process required listening to members, nonmembers, competitors, partners, staff, allied associations, customers of members, and leaders. Processes included focus groups, fax-back surveys, expert interviews, a competitive intelligence study, a town hall meeting, and private meetings with key groups.

The view for including so many perspectives was summed up by the current executive who continues to draw guidance from the plan: "Few things build trust more quickly than open, honest, and regular communications; and no aspect of the resulting dialogue is more critical than the art of listening, really listening by putting yourself in the other person's shoes."

Time was compressed into ten months for the entire planning process, but the commitment to work on short timeframes was outlined in advance and accepted by the task force, supportive staff, and officers. Tough recommendations were thoroughly debated and not decided upon until the debate was brought to conclusion. The task force required that consensus decisions ultimately receive full support from within its group even if the outcome differed from ideal personal preferences.

There were several key factors that could have been obstacles, but now serve as warning signals for leaders to overcome, to ensure success of a strategic planning effort.

Hostility to the Process

Some task force members were habitually action-oriented and wanted to skip various data collection efforts and wide-scope discussions. These participants wanted to quickly jump to the development of strategies and tactics for the long-range plan. They were successful in their own profession and businesses and had many years of experience as leaders in the organization. They felt that their experiences were sufficient from which to extrapolate the needs of the entire membership body.

Do you recognize these type of people? They want to rush to the action steps before understanding what the root cause or objective is. The result can be a waste of time and money implementing the wrong strategy or weak efforts toward an object that may not be a priority.

The planning consultant, however, was firmly committed to a broader and more in-depth thinking process, based upon many years of facilitating planning efforts. Many of the leaders also believed that taking a broader view of the industry's environment and actually asking stakeholders their opinions would deliver a more successful and on-target result. The other task force members also valued the larger perspective and did not assume they could speak for the large, diverse membership body without first learning more directly from them.

The consultant was repeatedly questioned by the same task force participants about the need for so much input and so much discussion because they wanted to get on with the task of finding solutions to what they felt were the most important challenges. The repeated and respectful response from the consultant was that the value of the broad input and comprehensive process would help them be prepared to make tough recommendations during later stages of the planning process. The goal was to deliver a comprehensive plan with deep implications to the future of the profession and the organization. The issues to address were not small; they were huge. The organization's executive understood the depth of the challenge. He also understood some members' fondness for data, research reports, and ongoing debate before decisions were made.

For example, tough issues to be explored included the adequacy of the professional training and preparation that members received in college; the culture and work style of members; the lack of inclusiveness within membership; and challenges of the governance and internal operating structure of the organization. All needed to be addressed in the strategic plan.

Fortunately, the leadership supported the planning process design, along with most of the task force members, and so they drove forward despite being frequently challenged as to the purpose of the process. Individual personalities and work styles had to be harnessed into a group outlook that would yield transformational recommendations with justification and clarity. By repeating on a regular basis how specific tasks fit into the total planning process, the consultant helped participants gain clarity to the importance and depth of the process overall.

Task Force Chairman Takes Ownership

During the early stages of planning, the consultant took the lead in explaining and facilitating the planning process. The chairman of the task force was the appointed leader making administrative decisions along the way, such as appointing sub-committees within the group, and also representing the task force to stakeholders at other meetings. However, it was important for the chairman to put his arms around the planning effort and take ownership to ensure his commitment to the process and the end result. Anything less than full ownership would be apparent during presentations, discussions, and implementation efforts.

After the data collection was completed, several lengthy exchanges occurred via email and telephone between the chairman, the staff liaison, and the consultant. For example, the chairman felt urgency for the task force to quickly define a new "vision" for the organization in order to guide early planning discussions.

A vision statement or scenario describes where the organization wants to be in the future after the strategic plan is successfully implemented. The vision is the desired future. Creating a consensus vision is one of the most challenging parts of planning.

The consultant emphasized the need to try to begin from a point of wonder and openness, to learn from stakeholders first and be willing to *not* quickly define a vision. Additionally, the scope of a mission statement was clarified to the chairman, explaining that they do not have to cure all the world's ills but just focus on the members and stakeholders that were affected. The mission statement describes the purpose for the organization's existence: Why are we are here; what do we focus on, and for whom?

Other private, thoughtful discussions with the chairman revolved around causes of problems verses just symptoms, diversity, hidden agendas, applying existing data in new ways, the role of facilitator, and specific deliverables of the planning process. This chairman was used to being hands-on in his daily life. He needed to understand in his own language the planning scope and the expectations for outcomes before he could buy in to the process. He soon needed to ask his questions. He did buy in as leader and spokesperson. He did it with his own folksy style and quiet intelligence. He took ownership and was committed to the process once he internalized how each step would help us succeed.

This is an important step for leaders to understand. To delegate and have others implement organizational goals with pride and success, the person or group must feel ownership of the goal. They must internalize it, relate to it, feel its importance.

Counterproductive Tangents: Stale Goals = Stale Results

Another challenge can occur when a group wants to wander down a path that may be counterproductive to the process or the task at hand. Participants in a group usually have a history to share and common experiences they want to discuss. While it is important for working groups to form bonds of trust, trust-building can be promoted through informal meals or planned social time together. In a strategic planning setting, too much history-based conversation can cause time delays in group productivity, and can actually prevent breakthroughs in forward thinking from occurring.

For example, this organization had a set of comprehensive goals established years earlier. The consultant purposefully did not want to bring these goals into discussion in the beginning of the planning process because these old goals could create blinders to new possibilities and new priorities.

The staff executive had instructed the consultant to push for transformational change; starting with a clean slate was one of the first process steps. Therefore, the consultant intended to go back at the end of the process to review old goals to ensure all bases had been covered, after the group had established its new focus based upon the new environment, new markets, and new competition.

A couple members of the task force, including the chairman, requested that the discussions for the new plan begin with the old goals. The consultant explained the benefit of starting with a clean slate to allow the group to identify what was really important given current issues and anticipated future trends. This approach would enable fresh connections and ideas, compared with thinking about old goals based on realities of years past. The consultant wanted any blinders off and old boundaries removed.

The request to refer to the old goals became more adamant during the first face-to-face planning retreat. Finally, the consultant did not want this difference in approach to turn into a power struggle or issue of dominance, especially with the chairman. Even though reading stale goals could influence or deliver stale results, the goal statements were read to the group, with one caveat. While the old goals were read, the task force was instructed to think about what had been learned from new data they had just reviewed, which included current industry and market trends, and competitive forces. Highlights from the data were posted on flipcharts on the walls.

The room became quiet. The old goals were read aloud by the consultant, slowly and evenly in a neutral voice. At the conclusion of reading the old goals, there was silence. Several who had requested the reading said "okay, we don't need these anymore," and filed the old goals away. They were never mentioned again. The group was back on target in creating a forward-thinking and responsive plan of action for the organization. They had confronted and deflected a potentially counterproductive tangent.

For leaders in this situation, it is important to stop and think about what action he/she can take to get a discussion back on track. Sometimes what appears as weakness or "giving in" in a confrontation is really just letting the other person speak and feel validated that they were listened to. Then, you can usually move forward with more willingness and openness to compromise or new ideas.

Forcing Follow-Through by Sharing Results

While collecting data earlier in the planning process, some controversial and uncomfortable trends about the profession and organization were uncovered. The input pointed to very difficult issues that needed to be addressed, such as weaknesses in the organizational culture, members' communication skills, traditions, and alliance relationships or lack of relationships.

It would be easy to understand if task force members wanted to discount the significance of such input, or to not identify that they might have been or may be part of the problem. However, many people knew the input was significant and it was on-target to explaining many of the fundamental challenges trying to be resolved. Most of the task force members and senior staff recognized the significance, even if they did not want to open the can of worms.

Fortunately, part of the planning process included "educating" members and stakeholders on what was learned from the data. Methods for sharing summaries of research results included information in newsletters, on the website, at meetings and in forums. There was no question that stakeholders needed to be brought into the planning process, especially if they were to understand and support recommendations for action that would come later.

So, the news went out on trends and patterns that were learned from various research sources. There was no emphasis given to any particular problem. However, the grassroots members caught on. The planning process would now take on a different tone, one of respect and difficulty. For the first time, the stakeholders understood that this would not be just a fluff and superficial exercise. The task force was facing tough issues that did not have easy answers. By sharing summaries of data, the word was out on what the task force would be addressing. They could not shy away from the challenges. Too many people were watching.

For example, six hundred members attended a town hall meeting to discuss key research findings and planning issues. They expected answers to their questions. The openness of the session helpe d the task force succeed in gaining grassroots respect and patience. The task force could not ignore the input received. They had to tackle very difficult subjects equipped with research information and broader perspectives. The diverse and representative data provided tools. The task force was quietly forced to reach consensus for the sake of the organization, issue guidelines through the strategic plan, and ultimately, to follow through on what stakeholders had told them.

Leadership that is inclusive can expect more support and success in achieving goals. The more controversial the prospective action, the more input and buy-in that is needed. In this case, the entity was looking to change the culture of a profession and organization, with new alliances, new rules for play, and new messages. Input and buy-in were imperative. Listening to the buzz at a grassroots level and addressing concerns and questions were key.

Wrap-Up to the Strategic Plan

Leadership made a commitment to the planning process, the players, and the outcome. This commitment was demonstrated by accessibility to top leaders by the task force for input and feedback, visibility of planning processes to stakeholders on a regular basis through newsletters and at national-to-local meetings, and sufficient allocation of funds and staff support. Leadership also gave public praise and recognition to task force members and immediately assigned implementation duties upon adoption of the plan.

Many issues were controversial and continue to be supported through new task force debates to hammer out details, implications, and solutions. The plan is a guide for the future. The task force designed the optimal scenario for success for the profession and the organization, using the extensive data collection and analysis undertaken. It is up to committees and staff to follow that blueprint and implement the strategies. Now, after several years have passed, the transformational vision still guides the group in setting priorities and achieving goals.

LESSONS LEARNED

- Continuously strive to remain relevant and forward-thinking for members, customers, and public audiences. This organization could easily have slipped into a passive position based upon its size and perceived strength. But the younger members and those on the fringe encouraged leaders to wake up and look at the competition and the direction needed for the profession.
- Old processes and traditions no longer work with new-world demands and new-world competition.
- Leadership is responsible for supporting appropriate platforms, venues, and people to ensure that successful transformations can occur.
- Leadership must be willing to address tough issues if the organization is to survive and thrive in the future.
- Leadership must take risks to open debates that could be very uncomfortable, but are necessary to move past obstacles. The process for debate must be examined carefully to ensure professional and constructive outcomes.

- Leadership must be willing to commit time, resources, and the organization's future to a planning design, and then ensure it is implemented.
- Think very carefully about who is appointed to lead task forces or implement major goals.
- Immediate and tangible actions, in terms of assignment of accountability and project schedules for implementation, are required to retain credibility and momentum.

The application of this case to other public and private entities can be found on many fronts. Perhaps one of the most important applications relates to leadership raising the bar of performance during times when things appear to be coasting along. If you are not moving forward, you are moving backward. Status quo doesn't exist. Moving forward may mean improving service, increasing relevancy, enriching the experience, investing in employee's professional growth, or experimenting with more creative methods.

Whether you use the process of strategic planning or periodic strategic thinking retreats, leaders win when they raise the bar of excellence, include diverse stakeholders, and invite others to question traditions in order to reach astounding performance.

⑩

ESSENCE OF AN EFFECTIVE LEADER: PERSONAL AND CULTURAL STYLES

THE FLY-ON-THE-WALL SPEAKS

For the last chapter of this book, I have covered a more ambiguous topic: personal styles of leadership and cultures of organizations, and how both style and culture can affect the organization's success. While many important attributes and styles were embodied in the previous case studies, some may not be obvious, thus requiring special attention.

Since leaders are people with personalities and varied histories, they naturally have a unique personal style attributed to their leadership that represents the complexities of the human being. Some leaders may be more aware of their personal style than others. Some styles are helpful and others are not. The same is true with organizational cultures. Some attributes of the culture help the organization and others do not. Let's look at several personal leadership styles and cultural attributes and their effect on the organization's success.

Respectfulness

A leader needs to be respected for his/her expertise, and also must demonstrate respect for others in order to be effective. It is a two-way street, and respectfulness goes a long way in building a cohesive and loyal team.

For example, one national organization in New York has elected leaders that truly listen and respect their staff's input. The sincere collaboration between leadership and staff is a unique asset that is too often not present at senior levels.

One observation at this N.Y. organization by the Fly-on-the-Wall is that when celebrating successes or solving challenges, the senior staff is not egocentric; they sincerely share in the glory and the problems. The harmful culture of territories, power plays, control, and silos of responsibility is not present here. Staff collaborates to address the bigger goals, and they respect the expertise that each player brings to the team.

The organization's executive stated, "Our staff is truly committed to the mission of the organization and believe in its importance to the U.S. economy. There is a culture of collaboration that places significant value on the input and contributions of all members of the staff." Respectfulness is a must for collaboration to work effectively.

A Quiet Thinker

Have you ever had a leader who is very quiet during meetings and you wonder if he/she is paying attention or knows what is going on? Well, I experienced that with the leader of a very important and controversial task force at an international association in Washington, D.C.

When I was concerned that the chairman of the task force was not paying attention during meetings, I later learned that that was just his personal style of leadership and thinking. What he was doing was letting the committee members try to solve the problem and generate creative solutions with commitment, while he quietly absorbed the conversation and his thoughts. He did not want to exert authority, bias, or control, which is admirable when collaboration is so critical to a successful outcome.

During meetings, the chairman would sometimes get out of his chair and move to the side of the room, standing and watching the debate. I was somewhat confused. Was the leader abdicating his responsibility? No, he just wanted to physically walk away from the table, watch, and absorb the discussion. He was adding in his thoughts and opinions silently.

After a while, I looked at him to see if he was engaged as a participant. You could not tell from his body language what he was thinking about. When he returned to the table and finally spoke, I knew that he was completely engaged. He was just a quiet thinker. He needed to digest his thoughts privately. He wanted the team to bond and work together.

When you are working with a leader that is a quiet thinker, give the space and time needed for collection of thoughts and digesting opinions. Some leaders are very verbal thinkers and others are not. Both can be effective, as long as others understand the leader's style and purpose.

Self-Confidence

You know self-confident leaders when you see them. When they enter a room, they have a certain presence. They appear composed and self-assured, with any signs of self-doubt spoken out of humility and respect, but still in a self-confident manner. Self-confident leaders look you in the eye and are not afraid to interact. Their style may be formal New England or casual Alabama—it doesn't matter. They demonstrate their poise through posture, voice, and message. It is a great asset for an organization to have a self-confident leader, one who can motivate staff, and provide a feeling of pride and purpose.

An executive in Washington, D.C. described one of her elected leaders of the international organization as such: "All of our leaders bring significant professional success to the table. Our past chairman of the board was very effective as a leader because of his comfort and ease in a variety of situations and in groups both large and small. He could talk to all members with knowledge, self-confidence, sincerity, and commitment."

Communication Skills

This one is obvious; however, a really effective communicator can make a world of difference in the organization's pursuit of success. Communication involves speaking and listening. Many leaders are criticized for one or the other. The weight of the message delivered from a leader's lips has much more at stake than some leaders realize. Their articulation of vision, strategy, risk, and opportunities can be received or rejected based on their communication style.

The art and act of listening must be genuine. Through both effective speaking and listening, the leader demonstrates his or her capacity to use intelligence and to receive intelligence from others. They demonstrate respect and sincerity.

Leaders can be naturally strong communicators or they can learn through mentors, media training, practice and professional development. One international association executive describes an elected leader with instinctive communication talents: "There is nothing more valuable than a leader who can deliver messages in a genuine, relaxed style. Having a leader who truly understands the issues and can present his or her views without relying on a script is a tremendous asset."

Ability to Lead a Meeting

Just because someone is a great visionary or intellectual genius does not make him or her a strong leader of a meeting. This can be one of my most frustrating moments, when the talent of staff or other leaders is gathered for a limited amount of time to accomplish important decision-making tasks and the meeting leader does not lead.

You probably recognize this situation. Even if an agenda has been prepared, the ineffective meeting leader does not call the meeting to order, does not follow the agenda, does not focus on the purpose of the meeting, does not officially adjourn the meeting (since many have slipped out of the room), and therefore, does not accomplish the work needed to be completed.

What a waste of resources and time! If a leader does not have strong meeting and organizational skills, then empower someone else to lead or facilitate the meeting. How many times have you witnessed the chaos of an unorganized meeting, when discussions go off on tangents, the meeting's purpose is forgotten, there is lack of control over loud or dominating voices, time extends beyond the agreed upon limit, participants feel frustrated, and a lack of productivity results? The real damage is that participants on the team do not want to attend another meeting with this leader, so you lose momentum and the effort can spiral downward.

Once again, leaders can add value by recognizing their strengths and weaknesses. Recruit others to take your place in certain situations or co-lead. Finally, listen carefully to constructive input; someone may be trying to tell you something that you don't necessarily recognize in yourself as part of your personal style.

Passive–Aggressive Behavior

This can be a difficult personality trait to recognize at first. The passive–aggressive leader may appear calm and not upset by things, but watch out, their disagreement can surface at times and places most unexpected.

I was meeting with a chairman of the board to review the goals for a strategy session involving his Board of Directors. We reviewed his purpose for the strategy session and the process I suggested we use during discussions. He listened, providing very little input, but indicated everything was fine and agreed to proceed.

During the heat of the Board meeting discussion the following week, there was wide disagreement as to the strategy to pursue for the organization. There was lack of consensus, yet we were at a point in the meeting where collaboration for a solution was critical. Instead of participating as a team player, the chairman remained quiet, showing no support or enthusiasm to help the group succeed.

Later, after the group had worked hard to identify and collaborate on a new more desirable strategy, they felt proud of their result and somewhat elated at what they had been able to accomplish. Instead of congratulating the team on a wonderful effort and appreciation of their time, the chairman's comment was "I almost walked out of here awhile ago. It sure was messy. I didn't think we could solve the problem. I guess we did, though." That was a very deflating remark. Everyone looked at each other with perplexed expressions. This was not a leader who motivates, or whom others are proud to have as a spokesperson.

There is a tendency with this personal style to be passive about ideas or suggestions, so that if something goes wrong they take no responsibility, and can, in fact, point fingers of blame elsewhere. It is better to strive to engage this type of leader by using his or her own words, by having the leader introduce strategies, and by having this leader take more ownership of both the good and the bad.

Ability to Fulfill Commitments

A large part of earning respect and trust involves fulfilling commitments. When leaders say they will follow up, take action, or do their homework, their credibility is immediately on the line. Fulfilling commitments is a personal trait that others will remember consistently. Leaders whom take responsibility for their words earn the respect and trust they need to be effective, by motivating others to fulfill commitments and instilling feelings of loyalty that may be needed now or later, for the good of the organization.

Constructive Energy

Some leaders have great energy and passion for what they do. When harnessed constructively, that energy can ignite transformational change within an organization. If the energy gets out of control, irreparable damage may result.

A leader of an organization had significant physical energy, running marathons at 60 years of age, while applying that same energy and persistence to his work. He had visionary ideas, loved to write his thoughts down and frequently shared his visions with others. His enthusiasm to lead the organization through breakthrough change and improvement was rewarded with being the right leader at the right time. Fortunately, his pattern of frequently sharing his vision with others proved to be his positive measure for how far to take his ideas and how quickly to move for implementation. He listened to the input from others, and without hesitation adjusted his course to allow for more time where needed, whether it was more time to gain support, more time for research, or more time to let political issues rest.

At the other end of the spectrum, I have seen leaders with high energy and enthusiasm who got themselves into trouble because of impulsive actions, hot heads, or not thinking of the big picture when pursuing a strategy. These types of leaders can greatly benefit from a colleague or assertive subordinate whom the leader trusts and respects, to advise him or her to slow down. Energy is a blessing when applied in a constructive way. Energy can be the downfall of an otherwise effective leader when it leads to a course of action that is not in the best interests of the organization at the right time.

Mentoring Future Leaders

The ultimate act of a visionary leader is to ensure the organization has a strong cadre of experienced future leaders. Mentoring takes time and cannot be completed by just one person. A leader should strive to be accessible to upcoming leaders and guide them to other strong players in the organization. An informal and sporadic coach and advisor can still go a long way to inspire young leaders, even if lengthy attention is not possible.

More structured mentoring and coaching can be a positive attribute of an organization's culture. I worked with an international entity that included very successful corporate leaders and entrepreneurs among their membership. The organization devoted a leadership retreat weekend to enhancing these already proven leaders' skills in mentoring and coaching. A speaker and expert coach offered key insights, which they immediately practiced on each other.

For example, the sometimes-overlooked practice of asking key questions that inspire action and commitment was practiced. Complimenting a colleague on action-oriented behavior, thus providing positive reinforcement, was also frequently applied during the weekend.

At the closing session of the retreat, the leaders individually verbalized a commitment to action that they would implement in coaching others with whom they worked. A leader who understands the significant long-term benefit of this type of retreat investment understands his or her duty and responsibility to the organization, to nurture future leaders.

FINAL MESSAGES

In the introduction of this book, the Fly-on-the-Wall mentioned that there were frequently patterns from which to learn the best and worst of leadership. Standing on their own, these final messages appear obvious and simplistic. However, taken in context of the case studies provided, they hopefully have a richer meaning and more helpful application.

- Listen to your gut instincts. If your instinct springs to alert when something feels wrong instead of right, or the answers received just don't make sense, respond to those instincts.
- Keep the big picture and longer-term goal as the prime focal point for actions and decisions.
- Listen first, and then take action. Test and validate ideas before moving too quickly. But do take action; don't stall forever. Inform others of when and why to expect action.
- Collaborate with others to maintain a full perspective and to receive greater buy-in and support.
- Use your strengths; empower others to fill in for weaknesses.
- What you see on the surface may only tell half the story, so dig deeper.
- Maintain a cool head and a steady hand. Professional, business-like behavior serves an important purpose for leadership at all times.

- Be willing to not control every idea in order to unleash greater commitment and creativity from others.
- Select your team players carefully; consider the integration and dynamics of the whole team together.
- Promote consensus by first defining it (the will of the majority; the support of all). Be a role model of support for consensus decisions.
- Promote constructive input from contrasting viewpoints by not judging or creating a culture of fear of reprisal.
- Be prepared; anticipate the opposing voice or outcome, and have a response or action plan ready.
- Constructively express your passion and commitment; it's motivating and contagious.
- Show respect for others and earn respect for yourself.

So what is the bottom line of all these leadership lessons?

When I think of what I would most want my young son to learn to be a strong, effective leader, what would I tell him, based on my experiences? Are the most effective leaders the smartest people, the geniuses? No, in fact, the brightest frequently have the greatest difficulty in communicating and working with others. Are the best leaders the smoothest slick talkers? No, competency, sincerity, and integrity must be present in addition to the ability to speak.

I believe the bottom-line advice for the best leader is to be an active team player, who can collaborate with others with integrity, in a sincere and enthusiastic manner, who can understand the big picture, and who can willingly share expertise while also learning from others. If we could all do that, the best of leadership would be achieved.

Best wishes on your leadership journey!

ABOUT THE AUTHOR

Nancy R. Daly's work with national and international not-for-profits and corporations has focused on strategic planning and consensus facilitation, leading Boards and executives to transform and provide breakthrough strategies for companies, professions, business cultures, and images.

Daly gained leadership expertise as a result of her own career achievements, beginning in the corporate financial services industry in national project management and strategic planning, transitioning to an international real estate organization as chief financial officer, and since 1994, serving a diverse client base at the executive level through her consulting firm.

Specialization in planning, and complex yet intuitive facilitation for collaboration and consensus building, has provided Daly with a unique perch from which to observe many different leaders and leadership situations. She is a frequent speaker and published writer who engages leaders and senior staff in explorations and discovery related to business goals and collaborative decision-making.

Daly also applies expert skills in analysis, planning, and facilitation to personal retreat settings where the empowerment of one's passion to make a difference in the workplace or world is the focus, and the

improvement of quality of life through personal transformation is frequently the result.

Daly is president of Daly Strategic Directions in Winter Park,
Florida. She grew up in Shreveport, Louisiana; graduated with a degree
in Finance with honors from the University of Florida in 1981, and received her Masters of Business Administration (MBA) from Florida At-
lantic University in Boca Raton.

Daly may be reached at Dailysmile@aol.com